Legends of the Ancient World: The Life and Legacy of Alexander the Great

By Charles River Editors

About Charles River Editors

About the Author

Tommaso Lagana is a History graduate from University College London who is currently pursuing a Master's degree in War Studies. In addition to having some of his works published in publications such as the Harvard Journal of Medieval Studies, he also writes fiction professionally and is in the final process of editing and eventually publishing a work of historical fiction.

Introduction

A bust of Alexander, at the Louvre

Alexander the Great (356-323 B.C.)

"There is nothing impossible to him that will but try" – Alexander

A lot of ink has been spilled covering the lives of history's most influential figures, but how much of the forest is lost for the trees? In Charles River Editors' Legends of the Ancient World series, readers can get caught up to speed on the lives of antiquity's most important men and women in the time it takes to finish a commute, while learning interesting facts long forgotten or never known.

Over the last 2,000 years, ambitious men have dreamed of forging vast empires and attaining eternal glory in battle, but of all the conquerors who took steps toward such dreams, none were ever as successful as antiquity's first great conqueror. Leaders of the 20th century hoped to rival Napoleon's accomplishments, while Napoleon aimed to emulate the accomplishments of Julius Caesar. But Caesar himself found inspiration in Alexander the Great (356-323 B.C.), the Macedonian King who managed to stretch an empire from Greece to the Himalayas in Asia at just 30 years old. It took less than 15 years for Alexander to conquer much of the known world.

As fate would have it, Alexander died of still unknown causes at the height of his conquests, when he was still in his early 30s. Although his empire was quickly divided, his legacy only grew, and Alexander became the stuff of legends even in his own time. Alexander was responsible for establishing 20 cities in his name across the world, most notably Alexandria in Egypt, and he was directly responsible for spreading Ancient Greek culture as far east as modern day India and other parts of Asia. For the ancient world, Alexander became the emblem of military greatness and accomplishment; it was reported that many of Rome's greatest leaders, including Pompey the Great, Augustus, and Caesar himself all visited Alexander's tomb in Alexandria, a mecca of sorts for antiquity's other leaders.

Legends of the Ancient World: The Life and Legacy of Alexander the Great provides an entertaining look at the facts and myths surrounding one of history's most famous men and conquerors, while exploring the lasting legacy he left on the ancient world and today's world. Along with pictures of important people, places, and events, you will learn about Alexander the Great like you never have before, in no time at all.

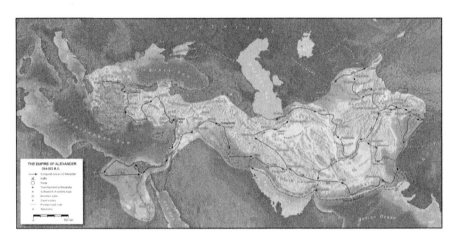

Alexander's empire at the time of his death in 323 BC.

Chapter 1: The Brightest Flame, 356-336 B.C.

Of the handful of rulers who, by right of conquest, have gone down in the annals of history as being worthy of the epithet "the Great", Alexander III of Macedonia is, perhaps, the greatest. In just over two decades he succeeded in creating the third largest Empire in recorded history (the second largest, if we consider only empires created by a single ruler) and established a legacy as a strategist, conqueror, and warrior philosopher that endures to this day. From his ascent to the throne of Macedon onwards he always appeared larger than life, endowed with superhuman abilities, a fact that Alexander himself took care to encourage, fomenting rumours of his divine parentage. As a result, he was a legendary figure in his own time, and he continues to be mentioned routinely in contemporary literature, music and film.

As a cautionary tale of the evils that *hubris* can bring about or as an example to look back upon – his attempts to pacify the unruly province of Bactria (modern Afghanistan) being especially relevant – Alexander remains a major source of inspiration for many contemporary politicians and thinkers. In a classic example of the light that is twice as bright burning only half as long, Alexander died under mysterious circumstances at the age of 32. Just what he could have achieved had he not died will never be known, but what is known is that Alexander was not even close to being finished when he died. It is believed he planned to invade the Arabian Peninsula, and he often talked of an invasion of Europe, a monumental task which, had he actually lived to carry it out, would have had unfathomable consequences for the entire course of Western history.

Alexander was born on 6 Hekatombeion (July) of 356 BC, in Pella, Macedonia. Pella was the ancient royal capital of the kingdom of Macedonia, a hardscrabble warrior state that had always existed, perched on the border between the Greek city states and the Balkans, on the brink between "civilised" Greek living and barbarianism. Alexander's mother was Olympias, a strong-willed and manipulative daughter of the King of Epirus, another Balkan state, and Philip II of Macedon, king of Macedonia.

That Alexander was even born is an amazing story in its own right, beginning with Philip II's incredibly unlikely rise to power. Though he was the son of a Macedonian King, Philip spent some of his early years in captivity, held prisoner in Thebes. Philip was something of a military genius in his own right, and after being freed from captivity, he succeeded in conquering much of northern Greece and repelling several enemy pretenders. His military victories were largely achieved as a result of his revolutionary Macedonian Phalanx, a tool which Alexander himself would later use to great effect. At the time, the chief strength of the Greek armies was their hoplite heavy infantry, strictly drilled soldiers who wore heavy bronze armour and fought with large round wood-and-bronze shields that covered over half their bodies. Hoplites traditionally fought with 9-foot spears, but Philip armed his own phalanx with 18-foot pikes, significantly outreaching the hoplites or, indeed, any other heavy infantry in the world at the time. Philip also developed another instrument of warfare that Alexander would later perfect, the Companion Cavalry, an elite mounted unit which would attack enemies on the flanks while the infantry pinned them in place.

Bust of Philip II of Macedon

Alexander came into the world dogged by rumor. According to popular belief, he was not the son of Philip, but of Zeus himself (a notion which mother Olympias doubtless encouraged). According to the chief sources for his life, the historians Plutarch, Arrian and Quintus Curtius Rufus, his birth was accompanied by great portents, but little is known of the earliest decade of his life – most likely because there is not much to tell. His father Philip was occupied expanding the kingdom of Macedon south and east, and Alexander was raised by a string of tutors. Because the Macedonian aristocracy, despite being looked down upon as boors by the more sophisticated Greeks, had pretensions of gentility, Alexander was tutored extensively in philosophy, oratory, history, music, riding, athletics and wrestling, as any young Greek nobleman would have been.

At the age of 10, Alexander started people talking for the first time since his birth when he accompanied his father to a horse fair. There, Philip was presented with a great Thessalian charger, but the horse was so aggressive it refused to be mounted, much to Philip's disgust. Alexander, however, realised that the horse was literally starting at shadows – chiefly its own. He quieted the horse and succeeded in mounting it, at which Philip is said to have told him, "find yourself a bigger kingdom than Macedonia, my son, for it is too small for your ambition". Obviously pleased with his son's impressive performance, Philip consented to buy the horse for Alexander, who named the beast Bucephalus, or "hard-head". Bucephalus was to be one of Alexander's most faithful companions, accompanying him on his conquest all the way to India.

19ᵗʰ century depiction of Alexander taming the wild horse.

Some years later, when Alexander was in his 13th year of age, Philip, still wishing to "Hellenise" (turn Greek) his son as much as possible, decided he needed a tutor. To coach the young Alexander he hired none other than the renowned philosopher Aristotle, a legend among Greek thinkers whose services he only managed to obtain after he promised to rebuild Aristotle's hometown of Stageira, repopulating it with freed slaves and pardoned exiles. Aristotle tutored Alexander in an academy, alongside his boyhood friends Ptolemy, Haephaestion and Kassander, who would later be his generals and play crucial roles in his conquests. It was during Aristotle's tutelage that Alexander became familiar with the Iliad, identifying himself especially with the mythical figure of Achilles, the mightiest of the Greek warriors, who was once offered a famous choice: long life and obscurity, or a premature death and fame that would last to the ends of history.

Ancient Bust of Aristotle

Portrait depicting Aristotle tutoring Alexander

After three years under the auspices of Aristotle, Alexander received his first chance to forge his own undying legacy when his father left Macedonia to wage war on Byzantion, leaving Alexander – aged 16 – as regent of Macedon. Philip's absence, and the presence of an untested ruler on the Macedonian throne, inspired several of Philip's subject and satellite states to revolt: the Thracians rose up in arms, but Alexander proved up to the task and crushed their forces, erecting the first of many "Alexandrias", the city of Alexandropolis in Thrace. Philip was extremely pleased with his son's performance and, in order to test his mettle further, when he returned from his campaign he dispatched Alexander, at the head of a small army, to pacify the remainder of Thrace. During this time, in 338 BC, Alexander also defeated a force sent from Illyria to attack Macedonia, as well as succeeding in his task of quelling the revolt in Thrace. He was summoned from the field with his army by Philip, who had used a flimsy pretext to involve himself in the affairs of the Greek city-states and was marching southwards at the head of the Macedonian army. Together, they marched through the pass at Thermopylae (where, years before, a Spartan army under King Leonidas and their Thespian allies had fought one of history's most famous and legendary battles against the Persian Empire, Greece's historic enemy), defeating the Theban garrison dispatched to stop them, and advanced into Greece proper.

Once in Greece, Philip and Alexander's main concerns were the powerful cities of Thebes and Athens, which had united their armies and resources against them. They marched on the city of Amphissa, whose citizens had begun tilling fields sacred to the oracle at Delphi, prompting Philip's invasion on the pretext he had been invited by concerned followers of the oracle. After forcing Amphissa to surrender, Philip sent Thebes and Athens a last offer of peace, but upon having it rejected, marched southwards. The Macedonian army marched quickly, but it found its path blocked by the Thebans and Athenians near Chaeronea. The Thebans were confident, having recently developed an outstanding martial tradition which had led to their vanquishing none other than the renowned Spartans, and battle was rapidly joined. Philip took command of the right wing of his army and gave the left to Alexander – cannily ensuring that his most seasoned generals were there to make sure the young boy did not blunder – and Alexander did not disappoint his father's trust. As Philip lured the enemy with a false retreat, Alexander personally led a cavalry charge that smashed through the Theban forces, instigating a general rout among the Athenian troops and forcing the Thebans, alone and surrounded, to surrender. The victorious Macedonians marched southwards, where they met no further resistance and were greeted with offers of alliance by all the major cities (save Sparta, which traditionally stood aloof from such matters). Philip united these cities in what became known as the League of Corinth, an all-Greek coalition formed with the express purpose of waging war on Persia, with Philip himself as *Hegemon*, or supreme commander.

It should have been Alexander's finest hour: he had proven himself in the field, he was the hero of Chaeronea, and he enjoyed the esteem of both his father and many of the leading Macedonian nobles. However, his triumph quickly turned sour. Shortly after returning to Pella, Philip set his wife Olympias aside in favour of the young Cleopatra, the niece of one of his generals. Alexander was furious at this, particularly as it jeopardised his position as Philip's heir, and he had a violent falling-out with his father during the wedding celebrations, to the point that the ever-volatile Philip actually drew his sword on his son. Philip was well and truly drunk by then, and succeeded only in sprawling on the floor, prompting Alexander to remark: "here is the man who you would have lead you against the Persians; he stumbles jumping from one seat to the next".

Following his quarrel with his father, Alexander was forced to flee Macedonia with Olympias, but he was recalled to court some six months after, Philip's anger having mellowed in his absence. Shortly thereafter Cleopatra gave birth to a son, also named Philip, which must have given Alexander cause for concern, and then the following year to a daughter. Yet Philip seems to have genuinely wanted to have Alexander succeed him, so much so that he wanted him by his side at a royal wedding celebration in 338 B.C. It was during these festivities that Pausanias, the captain of Philip's royal bodyguard, stabbed the king in the heart, killing him. Pausanias's motives were never established, though it his highly likely he was in Persian pay, as he was killed trying to escape. Whatever the reasons for his actions, Philip was dead. With Philip's other son only being a year old, there was no question who would succeed Philip. Alexander was proclaimed King by Philip's generals and the leading men in Macedonia. At age 20, he was ruler of Macedon and *Hegemon* of the League of Corinth.

Chapter 2: The Conqueror of Greece and Persia, 336-330 B.C.

"How great are the dangers I face to win a good name in Athens." – attributed to Alexander

Alexander's ascent to the throne of Macedon was not unopposed, however. Fearful of political rivals challenging the claim of a young and relatively untested monarch whose father had died so suddenly and mysteriously, Alexander had many of his political rivals, chief among them those who had a tenable claim to the throne, executed. Olympias, who had returned from exile, also took advantage of the turmoil to have Cleopatra, Philip's widow, and her daughter by him, burned alive. It is also likely that she tried to poison Philip's son by Cleopatra, but a botched attempt (or perhaps natural causes) made him mentally disabled, and thus no longer a threat. For his part, Alexander was furious at this barbarity, which prompted an estrangement which lasted for years.

Alexander also had to contend with problems outside of Macedonia. News of the *Hegemon's* death had not gone unnoticed, and virtually all of Philip's conquests rose up in arms: the Thracians, Thessalians, Athenians and Thebans all discarded their alliances with Macedon, rushing to occupy the passes in the north of Greece against Alexander's forces. Ignoring suggestions of a political solution to the uprising, Alexander led his cavalry on an encircling march around the Thessalian forces sent to bar his way, surrounding them and forcing them into surrender before marching southwards. The Greek city-states, terrified by the speed of his advantage, promptly sued for peace, recognising him as *Hegemon*. Alexander was formally invested with the title in the city of Corinth, where he also famously encountered the renowned philosopher Diogenes the Cynic. Alexander, who through his tutelage by Aristotle had developed an admiration for wise men, asked Diogenes if the King of Macedon might do anything for him. Diogenes, who was sitting in the public square at the time, sourly looked up at him and told Alexander that he could; he could get out of his sun. This remark prompted Alexander to later say, "If I could not be Alexander, I would be Diogenes". Plutarch would later write that Alexander and Diogenes died on the same day in 323 B.C.

A 16th century depiction of the famous encounter between Alexander and Diogenes

His position in Greece now secure, Alexander turned northwards, and in 335 B.C. he succeeded in securing his northern frontiers for good in a lightning campaign which crushed the armies of the Thracians and Illyrians utterly in a series of vicious battles. It was a remarkable display of soldiering, but one that the Greek cities seemed content to ignore: while Alexander was occupied in the Balkans, Thebes and Athens rose in revolt once more, despite their promises of friendship. Furious, Alexander marched his army southwards. This time, despite the entreaties of many of his advisors, he would show no mercy. When Thebes, abandoned by Athens, continued to resist him, he razed the city to the ground. This effectively ended all further resistance in Greece, and with his position as *Hegemon* firmly established, Alexander decided it was time to pursue his father's dream; it was time to invade Persia.

Ever since the famous Persian invasions that had been repelled by the Athenians at Marathon and then by the Spartans at Thermopylae and Plataea, Greece and Persia had been at odds. For the past few years they had enjoyed an uneasy peace, but that peace was shattered when, in 334 B.C., Alexander crossed the Hellespont into Persia. He brought with him an army of 50,000 infantry, 6,000 cavalry and a navy of over 100 ships, a mixed force of Macedonians, Greeks, Thracians and Illyrians, all chosen for their specific strengths (the Thessalians, for example, were famous cavalrymen). This mongrel force would become Alexander's *modus operandi* for the remainder of his campaigns.

Alexander's invasion was immediately challenged. At the Granicus, in modern Turkey, Alexander crushed a force of 30,000 Persian troops sent to oppose him, and during the battle he led the cavalry himself, as he was accustomed to doing. The destruction of this Persian field army granted him control of virtually all the neighbouring territory, and he captured the city of Sardis before marching on the fortress of Halicarnassus, which fell after a vicious siege. From there, he proceeded into Lycia and Pamphylia, systematically conquering all the coastal territory of Asia Minor. He then marched inland, where he famously visited the city of Gordium, seat of a renowned temple. The temple housed a cart whose parts were held together by a supposedly unsolvable knot, and legend had it that any man who could untie it would be made King of Asia. Alexander, disdaining any attempt at trying to fumble at the knot with his fingers, simply drew his sword and hacked it in two.

After wintering in Asia Minor, Alexander crossed into the Persian heartland in 333 B.C. Finally moved to action by what he at least perceived as a serious threat, the Persian emperor Darius III mustered an army that most sources suggest numbered almost 100,000 men, and marched against Alexander. Battle was joined at Issus, in November of 333 B.C. The battle was vicious, and Alexander lost more than 7,000 men, but he annihilated the Persian army, inflicting more than 20,000 casualties upon them and forcing them to flee the field. Darius escaped in the rout, but Alexander's men captured his royal treasury, his wife, daughters and mother. Alexander disdainfully refused an offer from Darius of a peace treaty and land concessions, claiming that as he was now King of Asia, it fell to him to decide how to dispose of his possessions. Alexander then marched into Syria, which he conquered with relative ease, but his attempts at pacifying the region in short order were frustrated first by the city of Tyre and then again by the stronghold of Gaza. Both cities had colossal fortifications that required the construction of siege works and engines of war on a scale hitherto unseen to reduce, and the resistance from both garrisons was exceedingly fierce, prompting Alexander to kill all men of fighting age and sell survivors into slavery when they were finally taken. At Gaza, as Alexander personally led an attack against the walls, he was struck by a missile from above and seriously injured in the shoulder, one of the many serious wounds he was to accrue in his time as a fighting King.

Mosaic depicting the Battle of Issus

Having witnessed the fate of Tyre and Gaza, the garrison of Jerusalem capitulated to Alexander without a fight, allowing him to push southwards into Egypt. The ancient kingdom of the Pharaohs had been reduced to a vassal state of Persia, and its inhabitants greeted Alexander like a liberator, the entire country falling to him without a fight. In 332 BC Alexander made a pilgrimage to the shrine of Siwa, in the Egyptian desert, where the Oracle proclaimed him ruler of the world and son of Ammon, the Egyptian patriarchal deity, leading Alexander to adopt the title "Son of Zeus Ammon". Coins minted by him, from there on out, showed him with ram's horns as a mark of his divine parentage. It is unclear whether Alexander truly believed the rumors of his own divinity, but it is undeniable that the Oracle's verdict severely inflated his pride, prompting the first accusations of *hubris* from his supporters, some of whom also grumbled that Alexander was getting dangerously close to going native. Alexander, unphased by these murmurings, journeyed to northern Egypt, where he founded Alexandria in Egypt, his most famous city. After letting his soldiers recuperate and receiving reinforcements, in 331 B.C. he struck eastwards and marched into Mesopotamia, the Persian heartland.

Darius once again marched to oppose him, but Alexander met his forces at Gaugamela and battle was once again joined. Darius had at his disposal anywhere between 100,000 and 250,000 men, while Alexander's force numbered less than 50,000, but once again the relentless machine of the Macedonian phalanx proved its worth by pinning down all of the superior Persian force and resisting all attempts to break through its lines, including attacks by war elephants and scythe-wheeled chariots. Meanwhile, Alexander led his Companion Cavalry and the Macedonian right wing in a flanking movement which outran its enemy pursuit and then struck straight for the center of the Persian formation, against Darius himself. The attack smashed through the Persian lines, causing the Persian center to crumble, and the entire Persian army was routed. Darius fled the field, but Alexander was unable to immediately pursue because his left flank, under general Parmenion, had been pushed back and was in danger of being overrun. This delay allowed Darius to escape, but his defeat was absolute: about 50,000 Persian dead, unknown numbers captured, and the entirety of their baggage train in Alexander's hands. Darius eluded Alexander's pursuit and vanished into the mountainous region of Ectebana (modern Iran). Abandoning his chase to consolidate his territorial gains, Alexander marched into Babylon, where he was acclaimed as a conquering hero. He then marched on Susa, where he captured the Imperial Persian treasury, thus endowing himself and his army with unimaginable wealth. Finally, Alexander advanced towards the royal capital, Persepolis. His way was contested by an enemy army at the Persian gate, but he smashed the enemy force and continued onwards, entering Persepolis in 330 B.C.

While he had entered Babylon peacefully, Alexander decided to make a statement in Persepolis. He allowed his troops to pillage the city for days on end, permitting them to finally take their revenge upon the hated Persian adversaries, and the palace of Xerxes, the famous Persian Emperor who had been defeated at Salamis and Plataea, was put to the torch. It is unclear whether this gesture was a deliberate insult, revenge for Xerxes ordering the burning the Acropolis of Athens, or whether it was the result of one of Alexander's famous drunken binges, but the end result was that the palace and much of the city were reduced to ash.

Alexander was now effectively the ruler of the whole Persian Empire, as well as king of Macedon and *Hegemon* of the League of Corinth besides. All of Asia Minor, the Middle-Eastern seaboard, and Egypt now owed him allegiance, but he wanted more. Prophecies in Jerusalem, Siwa, and Gordium had declared him the future King of Asia, and Alexander wanted to be ruler in name as well as in practice. This could never happen as long as Darius was still alive and still capable of rallying men to his banner, so after letting his army plunder their fill and rest in Persepolis, Alexander marched once more. He chased Darius farther eastwards, from Ectebana into Media, then into Parthia (Western Afghanistan). As Darius's supporters tallied his defeats, they began to slip away.

Eventually, the inevitable happened and Darius, alone and friendless, was deserted by his last troops and taken prisoner by Bessus, one of his generals and governor of Bactria (Central Afghanistan). Bessus kept Darius prisoner for a time as he continued to retreat from Alexander, but when the Macedonian troops threatened to overtake him Bessus had Darius murdered, and his body cast into a ditch. It is likely that Alexander, advancing with the Macedonian vanguard, found Darius dead, but he later claimed that Darius had been alive when he reached him, and had named him his successor. With Darius gone, Alexander could proclaim himself Great King of Persia, but his claim was threatened by a rival: Bessus, having murdered Darius, proclaimed himself Great King in turn and retreated into the heartland of Bactria, defying Alexander to challenge him. Such overt defiance could not be left unpunished: in 330 B.C., Alexander marched into Bactria at the head of his army, to crush Bessus and make himself King.

Alexander at Issus, as depicted in a Roman mosaic.

Chapter 3: Central Asia and the Indian Campaign, 330-324 B.C.

Many conquerors have entered Afghanistan with force, but few have been successful, and none would ever describe the region's pacification as easy. Alexander's incursion also came at considerable cost. With his veteran army, he pursued the pretender Bessus into Bactria, but even he was unprepared for the difficulties he was to face: the natives were hostile to a man, the terrain was either mountainous (and virtually impassable to all troops but light infantry) or a barren desert with no water or forage. Alexander reconfigured his army for the hostile terrain, shortening the pikes of his phalanx and lightening the armour of his heavy infantry and cavalry, but even that was not enough. For the first time, Alexander faced an enemy who stubbornly refused to be brought to battle. Bessus, who had been at Gaugamela, must have realised that he could never hope to face the relentless meat-grinder of the Macedonian war machine in open battle, so he decided to play to the strengths of his native Bactrian, Sogdianan and Scythian troops: he employed hit-and-run guerrilla tactics, dispersing his forces across the whole of the theater of war. Bessus never concentrated them in numbers sufficient for Alexander to pin them down and destroy them, instead striking out at isolated garrisons, baggage and supply convoys, and vulnerable detachments. Flying columns sent out to rescue beleaguered outposts were often ambushed, and with virtually every local, it seemed, either feeding Bessus's troops information or actively fighting alongside them, Alexander began to lose his temper. It was time for the Bactrians to reap the whirlwind.

Alexander scarcely needed to worry about public opinion with regards to his treatment of the hostile natives, especially where his Macedonian soldiers and generals, who considered them barely human, were concerned. He began to employ pacification by force: entire cities were razed to the ground and their inhabitants sold into slavery, to be rebuilt anew and colonised by veterans of the Macedonian army who were now disabled or too old for service for the most part. These former soldiers were offered large financial incentives to settle in the troubled province. Furthermore, whole regions were depopulated, with their inhabitants either driven out, sold into slavery or killed, and the regions were re-colonized with Persian subjects imported from the more tractable lands to the west. This virtual genocide was accompanied by the foundation of half a dozen cities to help pacify the surrounding lands, including Alexandria on the Jaxartes, and Alexandria Eschate ("The Furthermost") in what is now Tajikistan. At least one of them still stands today, and is one of the most important cities in the region – Kandahar.

The prolonged campaign, the miserable weather conditions, the hostile population and the constant grind of being forced to fight a seemingly invisible enemy while constantly worrying about receiving a knife in the back from supposedly pacified locals began to wear on Alexander's men. The progress of Alexander's conquests, which barring his great sieges had been lightning-fast, slowed to a crawl, and there was no guaranteeing that what had been conquered would actually *stay* conquered.

Dissension and disillusionment, not least with Alexander himself, were rife. Many of Alexander's generals openly advocated turning back to Mesopotamia, if not Macedonia itself, and there was growing concern, openly voiced – the Macedonian King famously being a first among equals, and thus open to criticism – about Alexander's "going native". He had begun to adopt certain elements of local dress and took the Persian title of *Shahanshah* ("King of Kings"), but what truly soured his generals against him was the adoption of the Persian custom of *proskynesis*. Quite what *proskynesis* was is unclear, but it is certain that it was some form of obeisance, a courtesy that the many Persian generals and courtiers now accompanying Alexander felt obliged to render him as befitted his title of King of Kings.

The Macedonian generals, however, were having none of it: obeisances were traditionally left to Gods alone, and this, coupled with Alexander's previous declaration that he was the son of Zeus Ammon, was seen as *hubris* of the highest degree. Tempers frayed, then finally snapped: at a banquet that year, Alexander infamously took a spear to Cleitus the Black, one of his generals, in a drunken brawl. Cleitus, who had saved Alexander's life at Gaugamela, had insulted Alexander's Persian courtiers, prompting Alexander to rise in fury and run him through.

Tortured with remorse, he took to his rooms and did not emerge for days: it was Alexander's darkest hour.

THE MURDER OF CLITUS.

Portrait depicting the death of Cleitus, by Andre Castaigne

For Alexander, there was no respite. There were at least two plots to assassinate him during this period, one of which implicated Alexander's general and boyhood friend Philotas, who was also the son of Parmenion, another general of Alexander's who had served with his father and had held the left at Gaugamela. Philotas was executed for his part in the plot and Parmenion, who had been left behind by Alexander at Ectebana, was assassinated to prevent reprisals. A further plot was uncovered later that year, this time involving Alexander's pages and his personal historian, Callisthenes. Increasingly beset by difficulties, it seemed as though Alexander's entire invasion of Bactria and the adjoining territories might unravel completely, with not even Bessus's betrayal and assassination in 329 BC serving as respite. When Bessus's own people captured him and turned him over, Alexander reportedly had his nose and ears cut off, which was an Ancient Persian custom for punished rebels. Ancient accounts conflict on how Bessus ultimately died, but they all agree that he was tortured in some fashion or another.

THE PUNISHMENT OF BESSUS.

Portrait of Bessus being crucified, by Andre Castaigne

If anything the man who took his place, the Bactrian Spitamenes, was even more resourceful and cunning than his predecessor, and it took an absolutely titanic amount of gold, men and vicious fighting (including the storming of scores of hill forts in terrain inaccessible to siege engines, during which Alexander received a serious wound) to finally defeat him. After the Battle of Gabai, where Alexander crossed a river on a huge craft in the face of a colossal arrow-storm and annihilated Spitamenes's levies, the Bactrian general was murdered by his own troops. There was peace at last.

It was an uneasy peace, however. Alexander knew this, and because he intended to press on still further eastwards, he knew he could not leave Bactria in his rear in a state of unrest, as it would compromise his lines of supply and communication, which were already stretched dangerously thin. Accordingly, in 328 B.C. he took as a wife the daughter of a powerful local chieftain, Roxana. This union angered many of Alexander's generals, Persian and Macedonian alike: the Macedonians felt that Alexander should marry a girl of noble Macedonian or Greek birth, and saw this as further proof of Alexander's going native; the Persians, who looked down upon the Afghans as second-class subjects, would have had him marry a girl of Persian royal blood. Alexander ignored them, however, knowing the importance of keeping Bactria compliant, and when he finally marched south and east he was accompanied by thousands of Bactrian and Sogdianan cavalry, implacable foes turned willing allies.

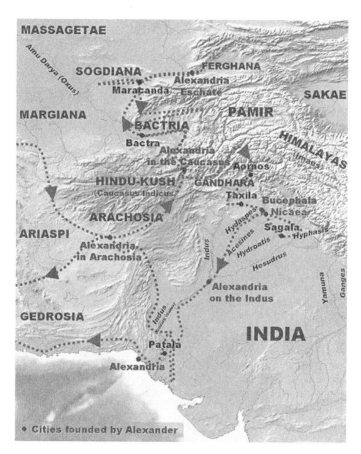

* Cities founded by Alexander

Alexander must have been glad to leave Bactria and its adjoining provinces at his back, but his troubles were far from over. Alexander was planning to march onwards, into India, and had made overtures to the wild tribesmen that inhabited the region that is now Pakistan, but he had been abruptly refused. The chieftains of the hill clans who guarded the passes of the mighty Hindu Kush mountains were determined to make a fight of it, secure in the knowledge that the high passes of their domains were virtually unconquerable. Alexander, never one to accept defiance, made his preparations and, in midwinter, a season traditionally reserved for rearmament and regrouping, he began his campaign. The Aspasioi, the Guraeans and the Assakenoi, inhabitants of the rocky valleys of north-western Pakistan, all opposed him, so Alexander destroyed their fortresses one by one, determined to extinguish them. The hill clans were fierce fighters, and each fortress, small though they generally were, was only carried by storm after days of vicious fighting which resulted in grievous losses among the Macedonian ranks. To give an idea of the brutality of this conflict, Alexander himself was seriously wounded twice during two separate sieges, taking a javelin through the shoulder fighting the Aspasioi and then a spear-thrust to the ankle in the assault against the Assakenoi fortress of Massaga. His reprisal was fierce: every fortress of the hill clans that did not surrender him was razed to the ground, and its inhabitants put to the sword, to the last man.

Despite the war-weariness of his veterans and many of his generals, after having vanquished the hill tribes Alexander pressed south and east into the Punjab. There he clashed with the most powerful enemy he had encountered since he had vanquished Darius at Gaugamela, the great Indian ruler Rajah Porus, whose domains included virtually the whole Punjab and who commanded an army tens of thousands strong. Alexander's force came face to face with Porus's army at the Hydaspes River, in 326 B.C. Despite Porus's strong defensive position, Alexander succeeded in forcing a crossing. When Porus threw forward his war elephants, the shock element of his force, Alexander's indomitable phalanx proved equal to the task: his men had faced war elephants before, and instead of bracing to resist their charge they opened their ranks, letting the beasts charge through, then encircled them and brought them and their riders down with their pikes. The phalanx then made short work of the lightly armoured Indian infantry, while Alexander's Companion Cavalry and allied horsemen drove the enemy skirmishers and horsemen from the field. Porus was captured still trying to fight, and Alexander was so impressed with his bravery that he made him governor of his previous kingdom, even going so far as to grant him additional lands.

It was also around this time that one of Alexander's oldest and closest companions, the mighty stallion Bucephalus, finally succumbed to the rigours of campaign and died, though it is unclear whether as a result of illness or a wound. Alexander was distraught at his loss as only a true cavalryman who has lived at his mount's side and shared his last morsel of food with him can be, and he ordered a great monument erected to Bucephalus, on the site of which he founded the city of – appropriately – Bucephala. Given the close association between Alexander and his horse, generals from around the world followed Alexander's lead and ensured that they used a favorite horse as well, from Julius Caesar to Robert E. Lee.

A coin from the Seleucid Empire depicting Bucephalus

Some viewed the death of Bucephalus as a sign from the gods that it was time for Alexander to go home, but he persisted on marching ever onwards, despite the fact that his army was exhausted. Many of his veterans had not seen their homes and their loved ones in over a decade, and the lines of supply and communication back to Macedon were stretched so perilously thin that it was unlikely that any reinforcements would be forthcoming. Moreover, Alexander's continual attempts to blend the Hellenistic and Persian cultures together, including the induction of Persian youths into the Companion Cavalry and his personal bodyguards, were souring his Greek and Macedonian soldiers against him. Finally, upon reaching the Hyphasis River, they could take it no more. They laid down their arms and refused to march another step eastwards.

Alexander raged, begged, entreated, and even threatened, but his soldiers had had enough. Further east lay still more powerful Indian kingdoms who, rumor had it, would await them on the eastern bank of the mighty river Ganges with hundreds of thousands of cavalry and infantry, and thousands of war elephants and charioteers besides. Alexander flew into a black rage, refusing all visitors for days, but eventually he relented, realizing that no matter how great their love for him might be, he could not persuade his veterans to march further south. After erecting a monument on the Hyphasis River to mark the easternmost edge, he at last turned his army westwards for the first time in almost 10 years.

The way back to Persia was fraught with peril, and Alexander's army suffered grievously. They encountered fierce resistance from local tribes along the Indus, and upon reaching the Persian Gulf Alexander dispatched the majority of his army into Iran, while he himself led a contingent through the desolate wasteland of the Gedrosian Desert, a barren and inhospitable region that virtually decimated his force. In 324 B.C. Alexander finally reached the Persian city of Susa, but the grim tally of his men told the tale of the price of glory all too clearly.

Chapter 4: "To the Strongest", 323 B.C.

Macedonian Tetradrachm depicting Alexander with Heracles's headgear, 336-325 B.C.

Factionalism, sloth, and greed had run rampant among many of the governors and other officials of the middle and high levels of Persian infrastructure whom Alexander had wisely chosen to largely leave in their place (rather than substitute them with men who had no idea what their job entailed). Doubtless many of them, when he had marched into Bactria, believed that he would never return, and accusations of bribery and corruption were rife. Thus, Alexander's progress to Susa was marked by a string of executions, as he rapidly made examples of the officials who displeased him. Once he reached the city, Alexander took good care of his beloved veterans: their back pay – which sometimes amounted to several years' worth of salary – was paid in full, with decorations and bonuses for all, and Alexander also promised he would ship injured and old veterans home under General Craterus, one of his ablest commanders. However, this last gesture seems to have been misconstrued by his men: perhaps they thought he wanted to replace the Macedonian units in his army entirely with Persian ones, since Persian youngsters were being taught to fight in the Macedonian phalanx formation. Certainly it cannot be that they did not wish to go home at last, not when they were finally so close.

Whatever their reasons, Alexander's men mutinied once again. For three days they refused to listen to reason, but this time Alexander seems to have greeted their balking with heartbreak rather than rage. It was only after Alexander threatened to appoint some of his Persian subjects to the rank of general and rename Persian regiments with titles properly belonging to old and sacred Macedonian units that his men relented. To show goodwill, Alexander feasted several thousand of his veterans, dining at their tables and making the rounds among them until late into the night. He also attempted to harmonize relationships between Macedonians and Persians by conducting a mass marriage between many of his officers and Persian noblewomen, though to little success. It is around this time that Alexander's closest boyhood friend, Hephaestion, died suddenly under mysterious circumstances, a blow from which Alexander never truly recovered. He grieved Hephaestion for days on end, refusing to leave his quarters.

Busts of Alexander (left) and Hephaestion

It was in action that Alexander found solace. Never a man to sit on his hands or rest upon his laurels, Alexander began planning his future campaigns, which may have included attempts to subdue the Arabian Peninsula or make another incursion into India. But fate had other plans for the young Macedonian king. One night, while feasting his admiral Nearchus, he drank too much and took to bed with a fever. At first, it seemed like the fever was merely a consequence of his excess, and there was not much concern for his health, but when a week had elapsed and there was still no sign of his getting better, his friends and generals began to grow concerned. The fever grew, consuming him to the point that he could barely speak. After two weeks, on June 11th, 323 B.C., Alexander the Great, King of Macedon, *Hegemon* of the League of Corinth, King of Kings, died.

The circumstances of Alexander's death are unclear. Certainly there were plenty of ambitious men, even among his inner circle, who might have wanted him dead, yet all of the main historians for Alexander's life discount the possibility of foul play, claiming no poison was used, and slow-acting venom capable of prolonging a man's agony for two weeks seems technologically unviable for the period in question. Perhaps Alexander was simply exhausted: he was a famous binge drinker, like his father, which did little for his health, and he had been on campaign for more than a decade, having sustained at least three serious wounds in the process. Even today scientists and doctors still try to diagnose Alexander based on accounts of his death, naming potential natural causes like malaria, typhoid fever, or meningitis.

On his deathbed, some historians claim that when he was pressed to name a successor, Alexander muttered that his empire should go "to the strongest". Other sources tell us that he passed his signet ring to his general Perdiccas, thereby naming him successor, but whatever his choices were or may have been, they were ignored. Alexander's generals, all of them with the loyalty of their own corps at their backs, would tear each other apart in a vicious internal struggle that lasted almost half a century before four factions emerged victorious: Macedonia, the Seleukid Empire in the east, the Kingdom of Pergamon in Asia Minor, and the Ptolemaic dynasty in Egypt. During the course of these wars, Alexander's only heir, the posthumously born Alexander IV, was murdered, extinguishing his bloodline for ever. And though it was unclear what killed Alexander, his subordinates were fully aware of the value of his body. According to ancient accounts, Ptolemy eventually took control of Alexander's body, and Alexander's sarcophagus eventually made its way to Alexandria, where it remained for at least the next 500 years.

Bust of Alexander's friend and general, Ptolemy

As the most famous man of history, Alexander's tomb was a must-see for the leaders of antiquity, and apparently his original gold sarcophagus was replaced with a glass casing, allowing his body to ve viewed. Ancient historians wrote some entertaining anecdotes of unknown veracity about certain leaders' visits to Alexander's tomb. Pompey the Great (who took the name Magnus and cut his hair based on Alexander) and Julius Caesar were said to have viewed Alexander's body without causing a stir, but historians claim that when Augustus visited Alexander's tomb, he accidentally knocked Alexander's nose off. And perhaps as a way to emphasize Caligula's insanity, historians claim the young Roman emperor took Alexander's breastplate for his own use. The last known date in which a Roman emperor visited Alexander's tomb was in 200 A.D, but it's unclear what happened to Alexander's body and tomb after that. The location of Alexander's body remains lost to history.

Despite the infighting among them, one thing Alexander's generals did agree upon was their Hellenistic culture. Most famously, Ptolemy's line firmly established the Hellenistic culture of the Greeks while ruling over Egypt. By marrying within their family line, the Ptolemaic pharaohs kept their Hellenistic heritage until the very end of Ptolemy's line, which died with Cleopatra in 30 B.C.

Alexander and his successors also succeeded in "Hellenizing" Persia and parts of Asia Minor, and their influence is still readily visible. Anthropologists have found that some of the earliest Buddha statues constructed in India bear an uncanny resemblance to Ancient Greek depictions of Apollo

This Buddha, with a combined Greco-Buddhist style, dates from the 1st-2nd century A.D.

Further west, much of Alexander's old empire was eventually conquered in the following centuries by Rome, including Cleopatra's Egypt. But instead of ending the Hellenistic culture, the Roman Empire further reinforced it. Having conquered Greece itself around 100 B.C., the Roman Empire heavily assimilated the Greeks' culture into its own. Latin was an offshoot of the Greeks' language, the Romans' mythology was nearly identical, and Roman poetry, literature and art all closely resembled what was produced to their east in the preceding centuries.

When Alexander died at the age of 32, he had made himself the most powerful man in the world. His dominions stretched from the Punjab to modern Albania, making him one of the most successful conquerors in recorded history. That he was brave to the point of recklessness is undoubted: he was on the front lines of every major battle his army ever fought. That he was a brilliant strategist who never lost a single battle is also out of the question, but much of his personal life remains fraught with mystery and speculation: some of our sources tell us he was handsome, tall, blond-haired; others that he was short, stocky, and with one dark eye and one blue. His relationship with his childhood companion Hephaestion has never been fully established, with some modern historians claiming that they were lovers and others discounting the theory. Was he a man given to excessive appetites, an arrogant hedonist who ruined himself with drink, food, and sex, as some claim, or the spartan, austere "first among equals" that others describe? Most likely we will never know the whole truth.

What remains certain, however, is that he profoundly changed the course of history forever. Quite aside from his own personal conquests, his successors went on to found empires that lasted for centuries, and local legend has it that the wild olive trees that grow in some regions of Afghanistan sprang from the olive seeds that Macedonian soldiers spat out on the march – not to mention the presence of Balkan features such as red hair and blue eyes among a significant amount of the locals there to this day. Legends of Alexander crop up amid the popular mythology of half the world, and while some among the Persian Empire called him "the accursed", it is now widely believed that the story of the prophet Dhul-Qarnayn ("The Two-Horned One") in the Qur'an is a reference to Alexander. However he is remembered, it's clear that no land Alexander set foot upon has ever truly forgotten him.

On the eve of the Battle of Gaugamela, Alexander's general Parmenion urged a diplomatic solution, telling Alexander he should negotiate with Darius and accept the generous terms the King of Kings was willing to provide. Alexander, it is said, simply smiled and replied, "And so I would if I were Parmenion. But I am Alexander, so I cannot."

In the end, for better or for worse, he was simply that: Alexander.

Bibliography

Readers interested in learning more about Alexander should refer to the highly readable ancient sources on his life, available for free on the internet or in annotated edition in most local bookshops:

Arrian, *Anabasis Alexandri*

Quintus Curtius Rufus, *Historia Alexandrii Magni*

Plutarch, *Life of Alexander the Great*

Those looking for a more up-to-date, comprehensive history of Alexander and his empire should consult Robin Lane Fox's excellent *Alexander the Great.*

Printed in Great Britain
by Amazon